GROUNDBREAKERS

Alexander Fleming

Steve Parker

Heinemann
LIBRARY

www.heinemann.co.uk

H Visit our website to find out more information about **Heinemann Library** books.

To order:

☎ Phone 44 (0) 1865 888066

📄 Send a fax to 44 (0) 1865 314091

💻 Visit the Heinemann Bookshop at www.heinemann.co.uk to browse our catalogue and order online.

Produced by Monkey Puzzle Media Ltd,
Gissing's Farm, Fressingfield, Suffolk IP21 5SH, UK

First published in Great Britain by Heinemann Library,
Halley Court, Jordan Hill, Oxford OX2 8EJ,
a division of Reed Educational and Professional Publishing Ltd.
Heinemann is a registered trademark of Reed Educational and Professional Publishing Ltd.

OXFORD MELBOURNE AUCKLAND
JOHANNESBURG BLANTYRE GABORONE
IBADAN PORTSMOUTH (NH) USA CHICAGO

Designed by Katrina ffiske
Illustrated by Michael Posen
Originated by Ambassador Litho Ltd
Printed in Hong Kong

ISBN 0 431 10477 8 (hardback)
05 04 03 02 01
10 9 8 7 6 5 4 3 2 1

British Library Cataloguing in Publication Data
Parker, Steve, 1952-
  Alexander Fleming. - (Groundbreakers)
  1.Fleming, Alexander, 1881-1955 - Juvenile literature 2.Bacteriologists - Great Britain - Biography - Juvenile literature 3.Penicillin - History - Juvenile literature
  I.Title
  616'.014'092

Acknowledgements

The publishers would like to thank the following for permission to reproduce photographs: AKG London 10, 32; Art Archive 9/Musée de versailles/Dagli Orti, 19, 37; Corbis 6; East Ayrshire Museum and Arts Council 7; Dr Robert Fleming 24; Hulton Getty 27; Imperial War Museum 23; London Scottish Regimental Trust 11; Mary Evans Picture Library 8, 17, 20; MPM Images 25, 33; Popperfoto 22, 40, 41; Science and Society Picture Library 4/DHA/NMPFT, 12/Science Museum, 18/Science Museum, 28/Science Museum, 36/DHA/NMPFT, 38/Science Museum, 39/Science Museum; Science Photo Library 5/Geoff Tompkinson, 13/St Mary's Hospital Medical School, 14/St Mary's Hospital Medical School, 15/St Mary's Hospital Medical School, 16/St Mary's Hospital Medical School, 29/Dr Jeremy Burgess, 30/Dr Jeremy Burgess, 31/Secchi-Lecaque/Roussel-UCLAF, 34, 42/Cordelia Molloy, 43/Martin Bond.

Cover photograph reproduced with the permission of Popperfoto.

Every effort has been made to contact copyright holders of any material reproduced in this book. Any omissions will be rectified in subsequent printings if notice is given to the publishers.

Any words appearing in the text in bold, **like this**, are explained in the glossary.

Contents

The man who saved millions

Every day around the world, millions of people have medical operations, or surgery. During or after surgery it is possible for tiny living things, known as germs, to get into the body through the surgical cut or incision, and multiply. The germs can cause an **infection**. Infection can also happen after an accident where the skin is broken by a cut or wound and gets dirty.

From the mid-1940s Alexander Fleming, with his trademark bow tie, was known around the world as one of the first 'medical superstars'.

The terrible risk of infection

Today the risks of infection are tiny. But about 60 years ago they were very serious. Indeed surgery was used much more rarely in those days because, in some cases, the person was less likely to get better after the operation and more likely to die from infection. In wars and conflicts, more soldiers died from infection of their injuries and wounds, than from the actual injuries themselves.

A chance discovery

Born in 1881 in Scotland, Alexander Fleming was one of the scientists who helped to change this. In 1928 he made one of the greatest discoveries in all of medicine, while working at St Mary's Hospital in London. Almost by accident, Fleming found a mysterious substance that killed microscopic germs, especially the types of germs known as **bacteria**, which cause many different kinds of infections. The substance was made by a type of natural mould or fungus, which grew as a fluffy layer on rotting fruit, soil and other items.

A researcher today using a computer to work on models of the structures of possible new drugs.

Worldwide fame

At the time, Fleming's marvellous discovery did not make world headlines. But through a series of chance events, other scientists began to work on the mysterious, mould-produced substance. They made it pure, tested it and showed that it was indeed an amazingly powerful germ-killer. Towards the end of World War II (1939–45) it was mass-produced and used to treat wounded soldiers, with incredible success. Fleming's chance discovery really did save millions of lives, and it has been doing so ever since.

This mysterious substance is **penicillin**. Its success made Alexander Fleming one of the most famous people in the world. He has been remembered by almost every nation on Earth. Even the Moon has a crater named after him.

ONGOING IMPACT   A new era in medicine

Penicillin is an **antibiotic** drug. Antibiotics harm or kill the types of germs known as bacteria. Since Fleming's time, many more antibiotics, now numbering more than 8000, have been discovered to treat many different kinds of infections. They have changed medicine so much that doctors speak of the 'pre-antibiotic era'. Before penicillin, infection was such a great and ever-present threat that it was one of the biggest killers. We live in the 'antibiotic era', when infection is less likely, and medicine is much safer.

Small beginnings

Alexander Fleming was born on 6 August 1881 at Lochfield, a hill farm in rugged moorland country near the town of Darvel, Ayrshire, in Scotland. His father Hugh ran the farm. Hugh Fleming had four children – Jane, Hugh, Tom and Mary – by his first wife, who had died in 1874. Two years later Hugh married Grace Morton. Together, they had four more children – Grace, John, Alexander and Robert.

When Alec was growing up children had to make their own entertainment. This photograph from that period shows boys who have been fishing in their local river.

Alexander was small for his age and known as 'Little Alec'. His main childhood friend was his younger brother, Robert. The whole family helped on their 300-hectare farm, where they raised sheep and cows, and grew hay and wheat.

Life on the farm

Lochfield was 6 kilometres (about 4 miles) across steep countryside from the nearest town, Darvel. There were no cars, and no radio or television when the Fleming children were growing up. In summer the youngsters played outdoors, catching trout in the streams and rabbits on the moors. 'Little Alec' soon showed that he was an excellent wildlife observer. He was also skilled with his hands, able to grab trout straight from the water. In winter the brothers and sisters devised their own pastimes. Alec enjoyed making new toys and funny games. His powers of memory and observation, and his ability to make things, would be useful in the future.

Lochfield Farm, Alec's birthplace and childhood home, as it was in the 1970s. The farm was rented by the Fleming family from the Earl of Loudoun.

Off to school

Alec attended the nearby village primary school, called Loudoun Moor. There were only 12 to 15 pupils, mostly from two or three local families. Alec was clever, and he did well at primary school without having to work too hard.

In 1888, when Alec was 7, his father died from a short illness at the age of 72. Alec's oldest stepbrother, Hugh, who was 24 years old, took over the running of the farm. In 1891 Alec moved to the secondary school at Darvel. It was a long walk there and back each day. Although he was small for his age, Alec grew strong and sturdy. At Darvel school he again obtained good results in lessons without having to work too hard. In a playground accident at Darvel, Alec broke his nose as he went around a corner and crashed into another boy.

In 1893 Alec left school at Darvel to attend a larger secondary school, Kilmarnock Academy. The large, busy town of Kilmarnock was about 50 kilometres (30 miles) from Alec's home in Lochfield. Alec stayed in Kilmarnock during the week with his aunt, and travelled home by train and horse-drawn carriage for weekends. Sometimes he missed the carriage and had to walk the last 10 kilometres (about 6 miles) to Lochfield. Again, at Kilmarnock he got good exam results without too much effort.

A move to London

At the beginning of the 20th century, motor vehicles were beginning to throng the streets of London, but there were still many horse-drawn carriages.

Alec's oldest stepbrother Hugh ran the farm at Lochfield but he could not support the growing family. Local jobs were scarce. Alec's second-oldest stepbrother Tom had trained to become a doctor and moved to London. Tom set up as an **oculist** at 144 Marylebone Road, examining people's eyes and prescribing spectacles. Their sister Mary went with him as housekeeper. In 1893 Tom suggested that his brother John should also move to London and become an apprentice lens-maker. The business began to prosper. In 1895 Tom asked Alec if he would like to come to London with its great opportunities for study and work. Alec was not quite 14 years old when he, too, left Kilmarnock Academy and moved south. Six months later Robert joined them, so there were four brothers and one sister in London.

Learning to keep quiet

In remote Scotland, the Flemings had always been a close family, supporting each other. They were the same in bustling London. Alec and then Robert went to the Regent Street Polytechnic School to continue their studies. Their Scottish education was ahead of English teaching and Alec moved up two classes in two weeks to be with much bigger, older boys. At first they laughed at Alec's strong Scottish accent, outdated clothes and what they saw as his strange, 'country bumpkin' manners. Alec quickly learned to speak only when necessary. However, the two Fleming brothers' quiet intelligence, helpfulness and sense of fun gradually won over their classmates.

Life in London

Alec and Robert walked for hours around the great sights of the city. They travelled on the new steam-powered Underground Railway and on horse-drawn 'general omnibuses' (buses). But they saw much poverty and illness in London's back streets and slums.

In the 1860s, Louis Pasteur's scientific skills helped to save the French wine industry from collapse.

Tom Fleming became a successful medical **oculist** and the family were able to move to a larger house at 29 York Street, just off Baker Street in London. Mary married and moved out, but Alec's sister Grace came down from Lochfield to take over housekeeping duties. After two years at the Regent Street Polytechnic, it was time for Alec to find a job.

Alec had no burning desire to follow any particular trade. Indeed, through his life he never had any great ambition. In 1897 he drifted into a job as office clerk to a shipping company, the American Line in London's Leadenhall Street. Alec's work involved filing and keeping the shipping company's records up to date. It was not a very interesting job, but nevertheless Alec worked hard and stayed there for four years.

In the army

British troops riding into battle in the South African War. Alec joined the army when the war broke out.

At the end of 1899 the South African (Boer) War broke out. In Britain young men were urged to join the armed forces. Loyal to their country, Alec and his brother John signed up in early 1900 as privates, low-ranking soldiers, in the London Scottish Regiment.

Robert followed them a few months later, as soon as he reached the age of 18. None of the Flemings saw war action or even went overseas. But they trained hard with their regiment, mainly part-time at evenings and weekends. After their childhood on the Scottish hills, the brothers coped easily with the long marches. Alec's helpful nature showed on a long train journey to Edinburgh. The carriage was so crowded that he, as the smallest soldier, volunteered to lie in the luggage rack all the way.

In the army Alec rapidly discovered that his fitness, strength, powers of concentration, sharp eyes and steady, skilled hands made him a fine sportsman. He learned to swim, joined the water polo team, won awards for rifle-shooting and took up golf. He remained a private in the London Scottish Regiment for 14 years, leaving only when his scientific work became too time-consuming.

A magazine cover showing the London Scottish Regiment, with Alec among them, marching to a rifle-shooting competition in 1908.

THE SOUTH AFRICAN (BOER) WAR

The South African, or Boer, War lasted from 1899 to 1902. The war was between two sets of European settlers in South Africa, over land and mineral resources, such as gold. The Boers, or Afrikaners, in the regions called Orange Free State and Transvaal, had Dutch ancestors. The British settlers and rulers occupied the neighbouring Cape colony. During the war thousands of soldiers arrived back in England, dead or dying from wounds and infections. The conflict was headline news and many people, including Alec, hoped for better medical treatment.

A medical student

In Fleming's words

Alec often spoke about medicine as teamwork and compared it to team sports such as water polo. In later years he told an audience of medical students:

'There are some people who think that medical students should spend all their time learning medicine and give up games. I don't agree... There is far more in medicine than mere book work. You have to know human nature. There is no better way to learn about human nature than by indulging in sports, more especially in team sports.'

In 1901 the four Fleming brothers each inherited a large sum of money, £250, after the death of an aged uncle, John Fleming, back in Darvel. This was one of many chance events which had a great effect on Alec's life. He talked to his brother Tom about what to do with the money. Tom suggested that Alec could spend his inheritance on training for a new career – perhaps medicine.

Passing exams

Alec gave up his office job. Before he could become a medical student, he had to pass exams recognized by the medical schools where doctors trained. So he went to the London College of **Preceptors** for more lessons. Once again he achieved good results, coming top in English and equal first in general proficiency. Alec also passed many other subjects, including algebra, English history, geography, arithmetic, geometry, French, Latin and scripture. Alec seemed to have the gift of predicting exam questions. He tried to think like an examiner, decide which topics would make good questions, and study mainly these. It cut down his work – and luckily for him, he was usually correct.

An operating theatre at about the time that Alec was studying medicine.

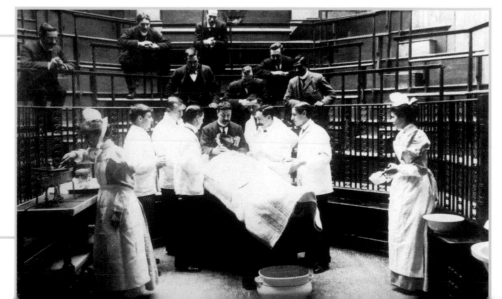

St Mary's Hospital, Alec's medical school. It was, and still is, one of the world's foremost medical treatment and teaching centres.

To St Mary's

Alec now had to choose a medical school. He remembered that, in the army, he had once played water polo against a team from St Mary's Hospital in Paddington, London. This hospital was within walking distance of his York Street home. This seemed as good a reason as any other to Alec. So in October 1901 he became a medical student at the Medical School attached to St Mary's Hospital. Alec's association with St Mary's would last for more than 50 years.

At last Alec had found a subject that interested him greatly. The idea of being a doctor fitted with his caring, helpful nature. He studied hard – but never too much – and excelled at his medical exams. He usually came first or second, swapping places with a student colleague, C. A. Pannett. Between them, they won most of St Mary's medals, prizes and awards. Pannett eventually became a leading surgeon. He and Alec remained lifelong friends.

Joining the team

Alec at work in the Inoculation Department of St Mary's Hospital.

In 1903 Alec's mother, Grace, followed her sons and daughters and moved from Lochfield to London. Alec, John and Robert lived with her at her house in Ealing, West London.

The following year Alec began to think about his medical speciality – which type of doctor he would become. He liked anatomy, the study of the parts and structure of the body. His skilled hands made him exceptional at surgical operations. So in 1905 he took the first in a series of exams to join the **Royal College of Surgeons**. As usual, he passed easily. The following summer Alec passed his main exams to become a qualified doctor and a Member of the Royal College of Surgeons (MRCS). He still had to get more surgical qualifications but he needed a job to earn money while he studied. He considered moving to another London hospital. But once again a simple chance event cropped up which affected the rest of his life.

A new job

Alec was an important member of St Mary's rifle-shooting team. So was a doctor and researcher at St Mary's, John Freeman. He saw that if Alec left for another hospital then the team would have less chance of winning an important cup that year. Freeman worked in the **Inoculation** Department of St Mary's, where new **vaccines** were made and tested. There was a vacancy for a junior assistant.

Here was a way to keep Fleming at St Mary's and in the team. Freeman spoke to the head of the department and in late summer 1906 Alec took the job of junior assistant.

The big boss

Almroth Wright was the Head of the Inoculation Department at St Mary's. He was a larger-than-life character in almost every way. In the year Fleming joined his department, Wright was **knighted** to become Sir Almroth Wright. He was also made a **Fellow of the Royal Society**, which is a great honour for any scientist. Wright had an enormous and lasting effect on Fleming's life and career. The two would become great friends, although there would be many disputes along the way.

SIR ALMROTH WRIGHT (1861–1947)

Almroth Wright was one of the most famous medical people of the time. He was a strong supporter of using inoculation to help the body's natural defences fight disease. He talked and wrote not only about medical topics such as the causes of disease and the need for inoculation, but about other great debates of the day, such as the role of royalty and whether women should be allowed to vote. He wrote many scientific and medical articles and also sent strongly worded letters to the newspapers. Wright inspired respect and occasionally fear in his colleagues.

Almroth Wright, Head of the Inoculation Department at the time Alec started work there.

The challenges of medicine

As Fleming began his work in the **Inoculation** Department of
St Mary's Hospital, in 1906, hospitals and medicine were very different
compared to today. One of the greatest problems was **infection** by
germs, especially **microscopic bacteria**. Today it is difficult for us to
imagine that infection was once so common and serious. But in
Fleming's time it killed thousands of people every week.

The problem of infection

A small cut or graze might become a breeding ground for germs.
They could quickly spread through the body and even threaten life.
Infection was a serious risk of surgery, too. Thanks to the pioneering
work of Joseph Lister, **antiseptics** had been in use since the 1860s.
They killed some of the germs on scissors, scalpel blades and other
surgical tools, on the bandages and other dressings used for patients,
and also in the cuts, or incisions, that the surgeon made in the body.
But infection was still a serious threat, especially in the few days
following an operation.

Growing germs

Fleming's work involved studying samples
of blood, pus and other substances taken
from patients. He would look through a
microscope at the samples and see which
bacteria and other germs they contained.
He would then add smears of the
samples to a substance called **culture
medium**, which encouraged the germs
to grow and multiply. The culture
medium might be a liquid in a flask, or a
jelly-like layer in a special small, shallow,
dish with a lid called a petri dish.

*Joseph Lister was one of the first surgeons to
use antiseptics, from the mid-1860s. Before his
time most doctors did not even understand the
need for clean hands during surgery.*

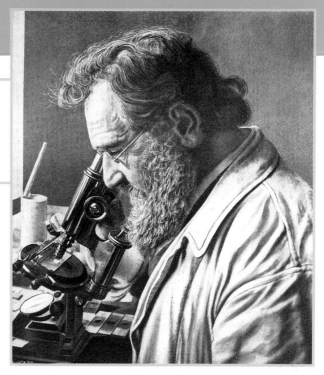

Ilya Mechnikov observed microscopic body cells surrounding and eating bacteria, as part of the body's defence against infection.

Different culture media containing slightly different ingredients encouraged different bacteria and other germs to grow. The individual bacteria were far too small to see. But as they multiplied into thousands and millions in the petri dish, they could be seen as small round coloured patches on the surface of the jelly. These patches were bacterial **colonies**. Fleming examined the colonies to find the exact identity of the bacteria, how they lived, and how they might be killed in the fight against infection.

ONGOING IMPACT Medical progress

In Fleming's time some of the recent advances in medicine included:
- development of **vaccines** or **inoculations** especially by Louis Pasteur (see page 9)
- the use of germ-killing substances, called antiseptics, during operations. English surgeon Joseph Lister (1827–1912) pioneered the use of antiseptics
- identifying bacteria by colouring or staining them with special chemicals, and showing which ones caused which diseases. The founder of this work was German researcher Robert Koch (1843–1910)
- the discovery that, in the human body, some microscopic cells called white blood cells 'eat' invading germs. This process, called **phagocytosis**, is part of the body's fight against infection. It was discovered by Russian-French scientist Ilya Mechnikov (1845–1916).

The Inoculation Department

In 1906 Alec's mother moved to a new house at 125 Clarence Gate Gardens, near Regent's Park. Again her sons moved with her. This house was convenient for St Mary's Hospital and Alec lived a settled life at home. He still attended the occasional London Scottish regiment event, and enjoyed taking part in quizzes, golf, snooker and table tennis matches, and played sports and games with his brothers.

THE FIRST INOCULATION

Inoculation was first tested scientifically by English doctor Edward Jenner (1749–1823). He used it to protect people against the terrible disease of **smallpox**, in 1796. Smallpox inoculation became widespread from about 1850. By Fleming's time there was active research into many kinds of vaccines against various diseases.

What is 'inoculation'?

At St Mary's Alec continued his laboratory work in the **Inoculation** Department. Inoculation or **vaccination** involves giving someone a vaccine, usually by injection. The vaccine contains dead or weakened versions of the **bacterial** germs, or their products, which cause a disease. The body becomes protected or immune to the germs without suffering the disease. Vaccination is a routine process today, given to millions of people each year.

In the early 1900s inoculation was the subject of great debate. Some doctors doubted it was effective. Almroth Wright was a strong supporter and his department aimed to develop better, safer vaccines. The workers grew bacteria, killed or weakened them with chemicals, tested them and sold the best vaccines to other hospitals and medical centres.

A stained-glass portrait of Edward Jenner, who used fluid from the sores of people with cowpox, a mild disease, to inoculate people against the much more severe disease of smallpox.

Fleming (in the white laboratory coat) with a group of colleagues from the Inoculation Department.

The career ladder

Alec was developing an interest in bacteria and vaccines but he still aimed to become a surgeon. In 1908 he obtained a further medical qualification of Bachelor of Medicine and Surgery, winning the London University Gold Medal for his excellent results. He also became a lecturer, teaching St Mary's medical students, a post he held until 1914, and he began to write medical and scientific articles. In 1908 he won a gold medal for his detailed account of how bacteria cause sudden **infections**, *The Diagnosis of Acute Bacterial Infection*.

Also in 1909 Alec became a part-time surgeon at St Mary's Hospital, carrying out small operations and helping with major ones. The next year his first reports and articles were published in the famous medical journals, or magazines, *The Lancet* and *The Practitioner*. Alec would write more than one hundred reports during his lifetime.

That year Alec also achieved one of the few definite aims he ever had. He became a **Fellow** (senior member) of the **Royal College of Surgeons**, FRCS. He was well and truly climbing the ladder of a successful career in medicine.

The 'magic bullet'

Alec worked hard in the **Inoculation** Department, where he was known as 'Little Flem'. In 1909 there came news of an important medical breakthrough. German medical scientist Paul Ehrlich (1854–1915), working in Berlin, had made a new kind of medical drug, 606 or Salvarsan. It was the first major drug to be produced in the chemical laboratory, rather than obtained from natural sources such as plants or animals. It was nicknamed the 'magic bullet' because it killed certain invading **bacteria** in the body without harming the body's own cells and parts.

By this time Fleming had another part-time job in a medical centre for **sexually transmitted diseases**. Salvarsan was effective against one of the diseases, **syphilis**. Fleming obtained supplies of the 'magic bullet' and used it with great success. But this went against Almroth Wright's faith in helping the body to fight its own battles using natural substances, rather than with laboratory-made chemicals. Wright and Fleming began to disagree about the direction that future medical research should take: would they try to improve the body's natural resistance to disease, or fight disease with chemically produced drugs?

Paul Ehrlich, who worked in many areas of medicine and helped to begin the science of immunology – the study of how the body protects itself against microbes and disease.

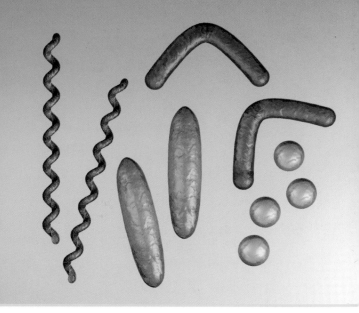

Alec worked on bacteria all his life. Under the microscope, the thousands of different types of bacteria can be grouped according to their shape: spirilli (corkscrew-shaped), cocci (ball-shaped), bacilli (rod-shaped), vibrio (comma- or V-shaped).

Life in the lab

The Inoculation Department at St Mary's Hospital was a small collection of crowded laboratories and workrooms known as 'the lab', where Almroth Wright was the undisputed boss. On a typical day the staff arrived promptly at 9 a.m. Fleming would set off on his ward round, seeing patients in the hospital. He checked and examined them and took samples of blood, saliva, pus from wounds and scrapings of skin. In the afternoon Alec grew bacteria in tubes and dishes and studied them under the microscope. Ever since he was a child Alec had been good at making things. He soon became expert at making specialist new equipment, especially pieces of glassware such as test tubes. In the late afternoon the lab staff assembled in their meeting room. Wright, seated in his large chair, made an opening remark about their research, or general medicine, or a piece of news. A lively discussion usually followed. Sometimes Fleming and the others did not leave until after midnight.

Social life

At work 'Little Flem' was still quiet and shy, but away from work he was widening his social life. Some of his patients were wealthy and powerful, and through them he developed new friendships, especially with famous artists of the time such as Fred Pegram and Ronald Gray. They invited him to the Chelsea Arts Club at 143 Old Church Street. Alec greatly enjoyed their company. From about 1912 he became a regular visitor at the club and then a member.

A SENSE OF FUN

Alec was usually quiet and serious, but he had a great sense of fun. In addition to making glass lab equipment he also made beautiful glass toys such as cats and dogs. He grew bacteria on dishes, not for work, but to make pretty patterns with their shapes and colours. He called these his 'germ paintings'.

World War I

In 1914 the outbreak of World War I shattered the regular routine of London life. Almroth Wright, who had once been an army doctor, was appointed as a colonel in the Royal Army Medical Corps. He took his staff and equipment from the lab in St Mary's and went to France. They set up a hospital in The Casino, a large building in the town of Boulogne, on the coast of northern France. 'Little Flem', by now a senior and respected researcher, was appointed as Wright's lieutenant.

Earlier, Wright had strongly suggested that soldiers were **vaccinated** against **typhoid**. This saved thousands of lives and the success greatly affected Alec. While in France Alec began to think of staying in vaccine research rather than becoming a surgeon. Also he saw that battlefield injuries, especially dirty wounds in the mud of the trenches, were still difficult to treat. The gigantic scale of the battles meant that tens of thousands of soldiers could be injured in one day, overwhelming the army's medical services. Soldiers often developed infections such as **septicaemia**, **tetanus** and **gangrene**. Even if skilled army surgeons could repair the wounds and injuries, infection usually claimed the soldier's life.

During World War I soldiers died in their thousands every day, often from later infection rather than actual wounds.

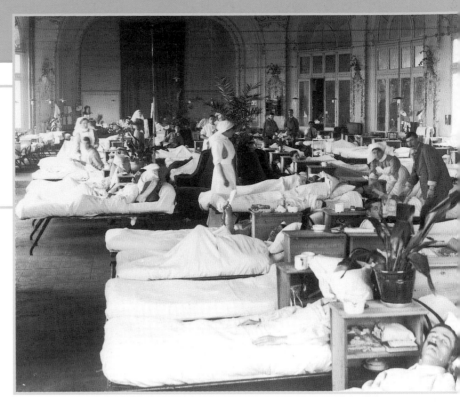

A large hall converted to a military hospital for injured troops in France during World War I.

Top-class research

Fleming was now a well-known **bacteria** expert, or **bacteriologist**. While attending to his soldier patients, he also carried out research into the bacteria in the soldiers' wounds. His idea was to see if **antiseptics**, widely used during operations to kill germs, really were effective. In a fine piece of medical research, which Fleming carried out while treating soldiers at The Casino, he combined results from laboratory experiments with tests on real people. He showed that antiseptics used in certain ways did more harm than good. The antiseptics destroyed many of the bacteria – but they also killed off some of the body's own defences, especially the white blood cells that 'ate', or destroyed, germs. It was better in some cases to use antiseptics sparingly and encourage the body to fight its own battle against germs, just as Wright always insisted.

Fleming also improved methods for putting blood from donors into patients. This process, called **blood transfusion**, is common today but it was new during World War I. Wright, Fleming and the medical team at the Boulogne Casino had other successes, too. Fleming was promoted to captain and received glowing reports.

A TIME OF PROGRESS

Medicine advanced quickly in the years during and soon after World War I. Blood **transfusions** became much safer, partly due to Alexander Fleming's work in France. **X-ray** equipment, invented in the 1890s, became more common and accurate. The bacteria that caused whooping cough were identified and a **vaccine** was developed against **Rocky Mountain spotted fever**. However, there was still the enormous problem of infection by bacteria after surgical operations as well as after accidental injuries.

A devoted couple

In 1915 while in the army, Alec went on leave from France, returned to London – and got married. It was a great surprise to almost everyone who knew him. His wife was Sarah 'Sally' McElroy. Sally ran a nursing home with her twin sister Elizabeth in Baker Street. This was near the Fleming family home in Clarence Gate Gardens. The Flemings and the McElroys had become friendly over the past year or so and romance blossomed. Alec and Sally were married on 23 December 1915. Soon afterwards Alec's brother John married Elizabeth, Sally's twin sister.

While Alec was quiet, shy and sometimes awkward, Sally was lively, talkative and confident. They were devoted to each other. After World War I Alec returned to his job at the **Inoculation** Department of St Mary's Hospital. He and Sally set up home in the flat in Clarence Gate Gardens, near the new home of John and Elizabeth.

The former 'Little Flem' was now a senior medical researcher and leading expert on **bacteria**. In 1919 Wright appointed him Assistant Director (second in charge) of the Inoculation Department. Alec's promotion meant more money, so he could afford to give up his spare-time work treating patients and focus on his research. Sally sold her nursing home business. The Flemings now had more free time. Alec liked to call in at the Chelsea Arts Club on most days after work, for a chat and a game of snooker, before returning home for the evening.

Alec and Sally were very happy together. They were married for thirty-four years. This picture shows them in 1944, on a visit to Belfast.

A country house

Alec and Sally often visited friends in the countryside. On a trip to Suffolk in 1921 they stayed with the Pegrams, Alec's friends from the

The Dhoon, Alec and Sally's country home in East Anglia. Many visitors came to stay and enjoy the peace and quiet.

Chelsea Arts Club. The Flemings had become interested in antiques and went to view some items at an auction in a house called Penny Royal, in Barton Mills. They ended up buying the house itself. Sally and Alec changed it's name to The Dhoon, and it became their country home. Sally often stayed and worked on the garden while Alec returned at weekends and holidays. They invited many friends and Alec loved to play croquet on the lawn and go fishing in the river, as he had done when he was a child.

ONGOING IMPACT   A new type of germ

In 1918 a serious form of the disease influenza, or 'flu, swept across the world, killing millions. Fleming tried to find the cause. But he could not track it down to any bacteria. It is now known that 'flu is due to a **virus**, a type of germ far smaller than bacteria, and too small to see with the microscopes of Fleming's time. However, Fleming's results were useful because they helped to guide research work away from bacteria and towards finding this new type of germ.

The puzzle of lysozyme

In the early 1920s St Mary's Hospital received a large donation from the University Grants Committee, an organization that helped to fund new areas in medicine and surgery. Now that St Mary's had this money to buy new equipment, it was time for reorganization. In 1921 the old **Inoculation** Department became the new **Pathology** and Research Department, with Wright at its head.

A germ-killer

At about this time Fleming began to work on the substance **lysozyme**. This is found throughout the natural world, in plants, animals and fungi (moulds), and in human body fluids such as tears, **mucus** and saliva. Fleming saw that lysozyme could harm, kill and dissolve various types of **bacteria**.

Fleming knew that bacteria are found everywhere – floating in air, on skin and clothes, in food and drink, on plants and in the soil. He realized that all living things must be able to protect themselves from most of the harmful bacteria. Otherwise the bacteria would be multiplying and threatening **infection** almost every minute.

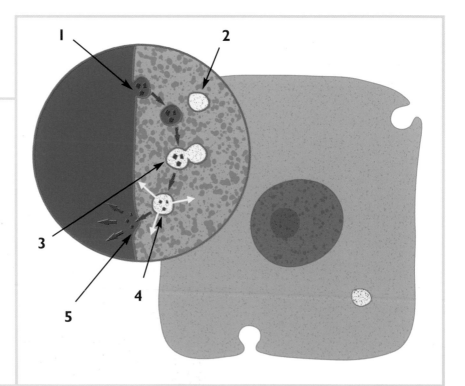

A living cell can take in or 'eat' bacteria (1). Inside the cell tiny bag-like lysosomes (2) release natural digestive chemicals called lysozymes (3). These dissolve the bacteria (4) and the leftovers are ejected (5).

A natural defence

The natural chemical called lysozyme was part of this defence. Fleming showed that it was effective against many bacteria causing minor infections. However, he found it was not effective against the really harmful and dangerous types of bacteria. This was partly to be expected. Bacteria that caused major infections could do so precisely because they were unaffected by lysozyme. Alec hoped to test more sources of lysozyme and find an unusually powerful version that would kill really harmful bacteria.

Fleming reported the results of his experiments at medical meetings. But few people took notice. As a public speaker Alec was nervous, lacked confidence and tended to mumble. His listeners became bored or turned their thoughts elsewhere. Further research showed that lysozyme was not as powerful as Alec had first thought. Gradually he lost enthusiasm.

In Fleming's words

When Alec first tested lysozyme, he was amazed at how it could dissolve bacteria: *'I put into a test tube a thick, milky suspension [tiny particles floating in liquid] of bacteria, added a drop of tear, and held the tube for a few seconds... The contents became perfectly clear. I had never seen anything like it.'*

A new town house

In 1922 Alec and Sally moved to a larger house in London, 20 Danvers Street. This was convenient for the Chelsea Arts Club and the Flemings became more involved with artists and art experts. Sally decided that she would now be known as Sareen, which sounded more Irish, to remind her of her ancestors. On 17 March 1924 she gave birth to a son, Robert. The Flemings' family life was very contented.

Fleming attended many social events such as the Chelsea Arts Club Ball. This photograph was taken at the ball in 1926.

The great discovery

PENICILLIUM MOULD

FROM PROFESSOR ALEXANDER FLEMING 1935

Mould grew as a pale, fluffy covering on one of Fleming's round petri dishes. The substance it produced killed nearby small spot-like groups of bacteria. Fleming noticed this effect and so began his great discovery.

In the late 1920s Fleming's research at St Mary's centred around how substances in human blood battled against **bacteria** and resisted disease. In July 1928 he received a great honour when he was appointed as Professor of **Bacteriology**. Just a few weeks later, Fleming made a momentous discovery.

Alec went off for his summer break to join his wife Sareen and son Robert at their country house, The Dhoon. But it seems that he had left some bacteria growing on **culture medium**, in petri dishes on the bench in his laboratory. He was interested in the way that the round patches or **colonies**, each containing millions of bacteria, changed colour as they grew. He wanted to find out if the colours showed that the bacteria were becoming more or less harmful.

HOW DID THE MOULD GET THERE?

There are many stories about how a mould had got on to the dish which Alec had prepared for bacteria. Some say that Alec left the lid off the dish near an open window and mould spores drifted in on the dusty London air, or that Alec sneezed over the dish as he was preparing it. Whatever the reason, Alec had the powers of observation to notice the effect of the mould and carry out closer study.

In early October Alec was back in his laboratory. He had stacked many of the petri dishes for cleaning. But one of his former assistants, D. M. Pryce, came by and Fleming gathered some of the dishes to show him. Fleming was suddenly struck by one of the dishes which had, not only bacteria, but also some type of mould growing on it. He put the dish aside to examine in more detail.

A brilliant observation

Alec had noticed that the dish had many round patches or colonies of bacteria on it, but around the area where the fluffier, lighter mould grew, the bacterial colonies were much smaller. Fleming reasoned that the mould might be producing some type of substance which affected, harmed or even killed the bacteria – the same hope he once had for **lysozyme**. The bacteria on the dish, *Staphylococcus*, caused sore throats, boils and other **infections** of the skin and body surfaces.

*Tiny seed-like spores of moulds, such as these **Penicillium** spores, float in the air almost everywhere. They are far too small to see with the naked eye: in this photograph they have been magnified over 10,000 times.*

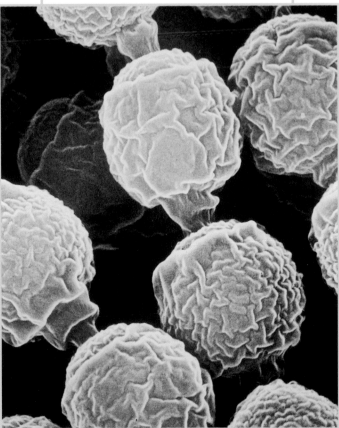

New hope

Moulds growing on dishes meant for bacteria were nothing new. Moulds grow from microscopic seed-like structures called **spores**. Like bacteria, mould spores float in the air and get almost everywhere. Research workers take many precautions to keep them away, but sometimes spores still interfere with experiments, especially if the equipment used is not clean enough. Usually Alec threw away mouldy dishes, but he knew that this one might be different.

Penicillin studied

Alexander Fleming was proud of his ability to notice small things that might one day be important. He showed the mouldy dish to his colleagues but they were not particularly excited. They were used to such sights after the 'false start' of **lysozyme**. A colleague from another laboratory at St Mary's identified the mould as a type of *Penicillium*. Its fluffy growths were common in soil and on rotting fruit. Alec took the name for the mould and altered it slightly to make a name for the mysterious germ-killing substance – **penicillin**.

Over the following months Fleming grew the mould in flasks and tubes. He poured off the liquid part of the mould growth, which he called 'mould juice', and tested it on various harmful **bacteria**. He was amazed to see that it was effective against many of them. It killed them or at least stopped their growth.

Further experiments

Alec also tested as many other moulds as he could find. This involved him in a strange search for rotting fruit, old clothes, animal droppings, dirt and muck. Alec's colleagues worried about his state of mind. But none of these other moulds had the same effect as the original *Penicillium,* from the *Staphylococcus* dish.

In fact this was another major piece of luck in Fleming's discovery. The mould on the dish just happened to be a natural type or strain of *Penicillium* with great bacteria-killing powers. If it had been a more ordinary, common strain of *Penicillium* then the whole discovery might never have happened.

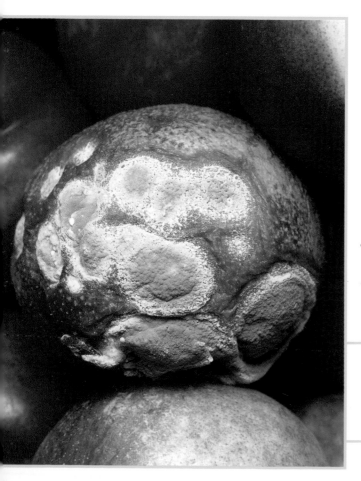

Penicillium *mould growing on the surface of a rotting nectarine.*

A promising start

Fleming grew more *Penicillium* and filtered the 'mould juice' to test it in various ways. It was important to show that penicillin was not only good at killing or disabling bacterial germs, but also that it was not toxic, or poisonous to people. Fleming injected the juice into animals. He washed the skin and eyes of human volunteers with it. He also mixed it with blood in test tubes, to see if it harmed the white blood cells (lymphocytes), which help the body's natural defences against **infection**. He even used it on one of his assistants to treat an infection, washing it into his nose and sinuses. The tests pointed to powerful action against many dangerous bacteria but few other harmful effects.

> *Microscopic blood cells such as this lymphocyte are part of the body's natural defence against bacteria. Penicillin did not affect these cells or interfere with the body's defences.*

In Fleming's words

Fleming became so excited about his penicillin 'mould juice' that he carried it around to show people, even away from work. A colleague described how Alec and Sareen visited them one Sunday and Alec pulled a slab-shaped glass container from his pocket. He showed the container to them with the words: *'From this slab will come things that will create world-wide interest.'* However, the others present agreed that it was *'only a dirty slab.'*

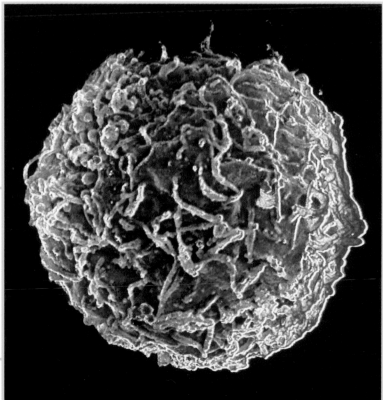

After his main work on penicillin in 1928–30, Fleming continued his laboratory studies on a variety of other topics through the 1930s.

Fleming continued his tests and experiments on **penicillin** into 1929. But he found it difficult to persuade anyone else that penicillin could be a new wonder drug. His boss Almroth Wright still believed that **vaccination** and similar methods to stimulate the body's natural defences were the best way forward. For him, this was preferable to attacking **bacterial** germs with artificial drugs such as Salvarsan, or even substances obtained from living things such as penicillin.

Fleming presented his results in 1929 to the **Medical Research Council**, the organization that oversees research into drugs and other medical matters in Britain. As with **lysozyme**, there was little support from the audience. Again this was partly due to Fleming's quiet and shy manner, and the way he announced his discovery.

The need for pure penicillin

Fleming needed to obtain penicillin in pure form to study its chemical make-up, find out how powerful it was, and show that it was active against bacteria but harmless to people. Only then could penicillin be tested on real patients.

However, penicillin was difficult to purify from its yellowish mould juice. Suitable scientists for this work were chemists and biochemists, not bacteria experts like Fleming. One of his assistants, Stuart Craddock, teamed up with another colleague, Frederick Ridley, who had worked with Fleming on lysozyme. They tried all kinds of methods, but at some stage of the process, the ability of penicillin to kill bacteria suddenly and mysteriously vanished.

The name 'antibiotic'

Fleming thought that penicillin might kill germs in the same way as **antiseptics**, by powerful chemical action. However, it worked more slowly than antiseptics, taking several hours rather than a few minutes. So he called it a slow-acting antiseptic. Then he began to use the name '**antibiotic**'.

Other chemists and scientists tried to make pure penicillin from the mould juice, but with no success. Fleming still believed that penicillin could be a new 'magic bullet' against **infection** by bacteria. But he had plenty of other work to do, not only research but also running the department. St Mary's Hospital was growing fast. In 1933 King George V opened the new medical school. Fleming was kept very busy.

> ### ONGOING IMPACT   Antibiotics
>
> The word antibiotic means 'against life'. It had been invented in 1889 to describe substances that prevented living things from working properly or that even killed them. The name is now used for the general group of drugs containing penicillin and similar substances that work against **microbes**, chiefly against bacteria and similar germs (but not **viruses**).

Modern drug researchers have many high-technology computerized aids, but they still use equipment such as microscopes, petri dishes and test tubes, which were in use in Fleming's time.

The wonder drug at last

During the 1930s Fleming worked on a variety of research topics. These included more experiments on his **bacteria**, such as *Staphylococcus*, and on **vaccines**, **antiseptics**, **lysozyme**, **penicillin** and treatments for illnesses such as 'flu and **pneumonia**. In 1932 he became President of the **Pathology** Section of the **Royal Society of Medicine**. His home life was happy and settled, at Danvers Street during the week and The Dhoon for weekends and holidays. Alec valued his relaxation time and spent happy hours playing games with his son Robert, who was away during term time at Stowe School.

Another 'magic bullet'

In 1932 in Wuppertal, Germany, scientist Gerhard Domagk discovered the second major 'magic bullet' drug, Prontosil Red. It was a laboratory-made chemical already in wide use as a dye. When injected, it cured **infection** by *Streptococcus* bacteria. The news spread and Fleming carried out some research on the so-called 'sulpha drug', reporting his results in 1938–40.

Howard Florey, one of the scientists who succeeded in purifying penicillin.

Pure at last

Meanwhile, penicillin had at last come to the notice of other medical scientists. In 1936 at Oxford University, Australian researcher Howard Florey (1898–1968) and German-born biochemist Ernst Boris Chain (1906–79) began to study lysozyme and eventually purify a version of it. They read scientific articles on lysozyme and other bacteria-killing substances, and read about penicillin, too. At this time they were not aware of Fleming's role in its discovery, nor was Fleming aware of their work.

1. Quick freezing

Flask

Mould juice

Deep-freeze mix

2. Drying

To vacuum pump

Deep-frozen mould juice

Desiccant

Refrigerator

Stages in the vacuum freeze-drying method used to make pure penicillin.

In their search for possible new medical drugs, Florey and Chain recognized that penicillin could be important, just as Fleming had done. In 1940, after many long and complicated experiments, they finally succeeded and made pure penicillin from the 'mould juice'. This was partly due to their greater knowledge of the chemical processes which happen inside living things. It was also due to a new laboratory technique called **vacuum freeze-drying** which had only just been developed. Fleming briefly visited Florey and Chain at Oxford and took a mild interest in their work but did not become closely involved in what they were doing.

Florey, Chain and their colleagues made enough pure penicillin to test on animals and then on a few human patients, in 1941–2. The results were amazing. Reports began to appear about yet another 'wonder drug'. But in the meantime World War II had begun in 1939. Scientists were urged to help the war effort. Penicillin seemed a great hope for the future, but money and equipment to make larger quantities of it were very scarce.

A NEW TECHNIQUE

Vacuum freeze-drying is a method of removing unwanted substances from a mixture to leave a single pure substance as a solid. First, the liquid mixture is quick-frozen to a very low temperature, minus 50 °C or less, by placing it in a special deep-freezer or freezing substance. Then, the deep-frozen mixture is put into a container. The air inside is sucked out using a pump to create an airless atmosphere, or vacuum. The unwanted substances 'dry' away into the vacuum. They turn into gases and are sucked out of the container. Water is absorbed by another substance or drying agent in the container called a desiccant. The wanted substance is left as a pure solid.

A great new weapon

Fleming continued his work at St Mary's, as best he could in wartime London. His Danvers Street home was damaged by bombing and he had to move to a colleague's house in Highgate. Sareen and Robert stayed at The Dhoon, the family home in Suffolk.

Meanwhile Florey and Chain were trying to raise interest and funds so that **penicillin** could be mass-produced. They were making small quantities at the Dunn School in Oxford where they worked, but not enough for proper patient tests. In 1941 Florey went to the USA and persuaded the American government to set up a small 'penicillin factory' at Peoria, Illinois, then a larger one at the site of the drug company Merck in Rahway, New Jersey. Penicillin tests on patients continued with great success.

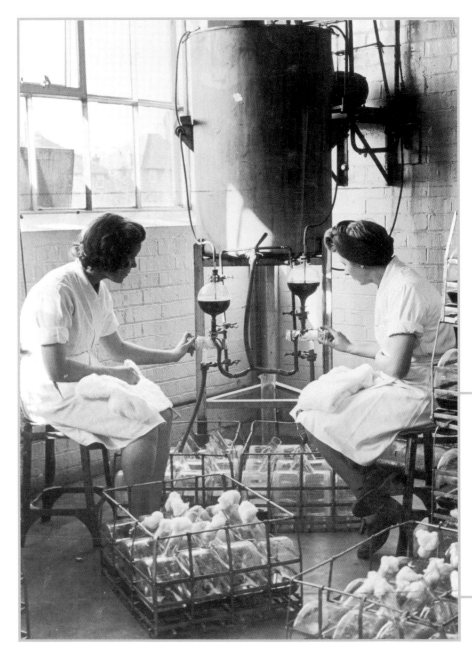

Penicillin 'mould juice' was grown in large vats and purified for tests on patients, on a small scale in Oxford in 1941 and then in larger amounts in the USA from 1942.

From its first large-scale trials on troops in World War II, beginning in 1943, penicillin was a massive success at preventing or treating infection.

A better mould

The method of growing **Penicillium** mould, like its discovery, owed something to chance and luck. '**Corn-steep liquor**' was made during the manufacture of large quantities of starch from maize crops. This substance proved ideal as a **culture medium** for growing the mould, just like a factory version of the test tubes in Fleming's laboratory 13 years earlier. Florey and Chain also added their own improvements to the procedure. They even found another strain of the mould in a rotting melon which yielded more penicillin.

Another patient saved

Medical experts and then the public became aware of the huge success of penicillin. In early August 1942 Fleming himself, still largely unrecognized as its discoverer, asked for supplies of the drug. He wanted to treat a patient who worked for the spectacle and lens company J. and R. Fleming, set up by his brothers. Again the results were astonishing.

The newspapers began to print letters and stories about the latest wonder drug. But still the general public did not seem to know how penicillin had been discovered.

HELPING TO SAVE THE WAR

Mass production of penicillin began in earnest in the USA in 1943. Its first large-scale use was for soldiers in North Africa who had infected wounds in the hot, fly-ridden conditions. It saved thousands of lives almost at once. Its use spread and by the end of World War II, in 1945, it was the most effective life-saving drug in the world.

- In June 1943 enough penicillin was produced to treat 170 patients per month.
- In June 1944 this had risen to 40,000 patients each month.
- By June 1945 the rate was 250,000 patients every month.

Fame at last

It was Alexander Fleming's boss who finally made sure that Alec was recognized as the discoverer of **penicillin**. On 31 August 1942 Sir Almroth Wright wrote to *The Times* of London stating that the credit '...should be decreed to Professor Alexander Fleming of this laboratory. For he is the discoverer of penicillin and was the author also of the original suggestion that this substance might prove to have important applications in medicine.' From that day the life of 'Little Flem' would never be the same.

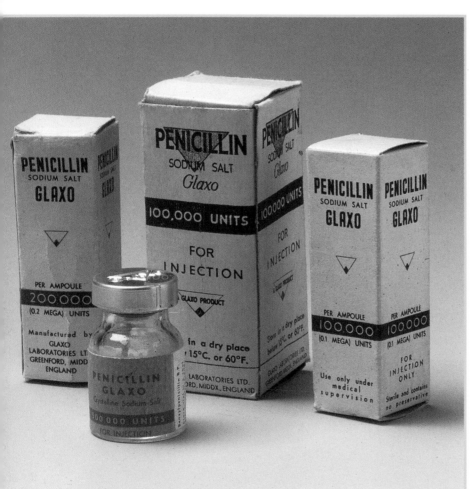

Penicillin was packaged in various forms and quantities, for use on different diseases and on patients of various ages. It could be injected or taken by mouth as tablets or capsules.

Penicillin's incredible success made the shy, reserved Alexander Fleming into a world champion. Suddenly he was the subject of hundreds of newspaper stories, magazine articles and radio and television programmes. The extraordinary story of penicillin's discovery, and Fleming's own career littered with chance events, led to many myths. One myth said that Fleming had risen from a poverty-stricken childhood in darkest Scotland, where he walked barefoot for hours to school each day, to become a world-famous scientist who, alone, had discovered, purified and tested penicillin almost with his bare hands.

Known around the globe

Fleming quietly accepted his part of the credit for the success of penicillin, but he was always careful to mention the work done by Florey, Chain and other scientists and doctors. However, Florey, especially, was less keen to receive attention. Florey disliked personal publicity and distrusted journalists. Furthermore, the tale of how Fleming discovered penicillin was easier for people to understand than the complicated chemistry of Florey and Chain. So Fleming became the hero of the hour.

Fleming received many awards, honours and titles in the years following penicillin's early success. He was elected a **Fellow of the Royal Society** in 1943 and was **knighted** as Sir Alexander Fleming in 1944. The honours rose to some 25 university degrees, 26 medals, 18 prizes, 13 decorations and membership of 87 scientific organizations and academies. He also received the honour of being made a Freeman, or honoured citizen, of Paddington in London, where St Mary's is situated. He became a Freeman of Darvel in Scotland, and later of Chelsea in the part of London where he lived.

In 1945 Fleming, Florey and Chain jointly received the **Nobel Prize** for physiology or medicine. This was, and still is, the leading global award for any scientist. Fleming had received the honour that most scientists can only dream of.

The Nobel Prize medal awarded to Fleming on 25 October 1945 was the greatest recognition for any scientist. At the same time World War II was coming to a close.

Great man of medical science

From the mid-1940s Alexander Fleming was busy with triumphant trips, tours and visits all over the world. He had improved as a public speaker and was in great demand. Also around that time other **antibiotics** appeared. In 1943 Russian-American scientist Selman Waksman (1888–1973) discovered **streptomycin**, produced by another type of mould or fungus, *Streptomyces*. This was the first drug treatment for **tuberculosis**.

In 1946 Alec was saddened when his long-time boss, friend and occasional opponent Almroth Wright retired. He was even more upset when Wright died, aged 85, the following year. In the meantime Fleming's own career rushed onwards. He became Principal (leader) of the **Institute of Bacteriology** in 1946 and Director of the Wright-Fleming Institute at St Mary's Hospital in 1947. Fleming himself greatly valued the medal from the **Pasteur Institute** research centre in France, which he received in September 1946.

Fleming carried by students at the University of Edinburgh where he was appointed as Lord Rector in 1951.

In mid-1949 Alec had the honour of meeting the Pope at the Vatican in Rome, and US President Truman at the White House, Washington, D.C. But later that same year Sareen Fleming died after a fairly short illness. Alec, who was 68 years old at the time, was devastated. They had been a close and loving couple for 34 years. Fleming became very withdrawn. His friends worried for his health and state of mind. But eventually he threw himself back into his work and also spent more time at the Chelsea Arts Club. He was also helped by his globe-trotting visits and tours.

The later years

In 1953 Alec married again. His wife was Dr Amalia Voureka, a Greek doctor who had come to St Mary's in 1946 to work as a researcher. After Sareen's death, Amalia and Alec became very close. Alec had proposed to her in 1952 after a visit to Greece. He was enchanted by the beauty and warmth of the Greek landscape and people.

Later that year, Alec suffered from **pneumonia** – which was cured with **penicillin**. He resigned as Principal of the Institute of Bacteriology in 1955 but he kept his own laboratory at St Mary's to 'potter about', as he put it. At the age of 73, he still went on tours around the world and seemed fit and active, when he died suddenly of a heart problem on the morning of 11 March 1955.

Alexander Fleming was buried at St Paul's Cathedral, London alongside other great British heroes. He was remembered with national and international honours, and mourned by millions as the man whose discovery saved their lives.

Fleming's legacy

Countless people owe their lives to penicillin, one of most successful drugs and greatest medical advances the world has ever seen.

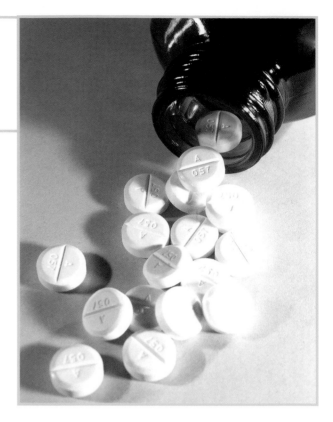

At Fleming's funeral, his old medical student friend C. A. Pannett said that Fleming, 'by his work… has saved more lives and relieved more suffering… than perhaps any man who has ever lived.' The Alexander Fleming Laboratory Museum was opened in 1993 by St Mary's Hospital Trust. Research continues today to find new and better **antibiotics**. It is a huge industry – based on Fleming's discovery of a mouldy dish on a laboratory bench.

ONGOING IMPACT Antibiotic resistance

In 1946 Fleming had suggested that some bacteria might become unaffected by antibiotics such as penicillin. The bacteria multiply and change so rapidly, every 15–20 minutes, that resistant types or strains appear. This happens especially if the antibiotic doses are too low or given for too short a time. This has indeed happened and new 'superbugs' now occur which are resistant to most antibiotics. There is a continuing need for new, better antibiotics and for great care and caution in using them.

Luck, genius, or both?

But was Fleming really a brilliant medical scientist – or was he just lucky? Probably both. If he had not discovered penicillin, then he would still be remembered as an outstanding expert on **bacteria** and other germs, and how to treat infections caused by them. If the mouldy dish of 1928 had been seen by someone without Fleming's keen eyes, powers of observation and great interest in odd events, then penicillin might never have been discovered. It is often said that success favours those with foresight. Would another research scientist have been so 'lucky'?

After the success of penicillin, medical scientists began to test many similar moulds or fungi, and other kinds of living things, in the search for powerful germ-killing substances. The work continues today. Modern researchers use incredibly accurate equipment. Computers 'design' new drugs on screen, chemists make them in the lab, and **genetic engineering** methods can mass-produce them inside living things. The industry in medical drugs, or pharmaceuticals, is worth more than £300 billion each year.

Alexander Fleming's extraordinary discovery has had a huge impact on medicine. Through the use of antibiotics, medical treatment has greatly improved. Infections that would once have been life-threatening can now be treated more easily. Fleming's discovery of **penicillin**, and the development of antibiotics is seen as one of the great medical advances of the last century. This wonder drug has saved the lives of literally millions of people. It is perhaps not surprising that Fleming has become a heroic figure in medical history.

Celebrated in stained glass at St James's Church, Paddington, Fleming is shown in his laboratory workroom, deep in study of his 'beloved moulds and microbes'.

Timeline

1881	Alexander Fleming is born at Lochfield, Ayrshire, Scotland.
1886	'Little Alec' attends the local primary school, Loudoun Moor.
1891	Alec goes on to secondary school at Darvel.
1893	Alec moves to senior school, Kilmarnock Academy.
1895	Alec leaves Scotland to live with his older stepbrother Tom in Marylebone Road, London. He attends Regent Street Polytechnic School.
1897	Fleming takes an office job at American Line shipping offices.
1900	Outbreak of the South African (Boer) War.
1901	Fleming studies for medical school entrance exams at London College of Preceptors, and enters St Mary's Hospital Medical School as a medical student.
1903	Fleming's mother moves to London and he joins her and his brothers John and Robert to live in Ealing, West London.
1906	Fleming becomes a fully qualified doctor and joins the Inoculation Department of St Mary's Hospital as a junior assistant.
1909	Fleming is elected a Fellow of the Royal College of Surgeons (FRCS). Paul Ehrlich discovers 'magic bullet' drug 606/Salvarsan.
1914	Outbreak of World War I, Fleming joins an Army medical unit.
1915	Fleming marries Sarah (Sally/Sareen).
1918	World War I ends.
1919	Fleming becomes assistant director of the Inoculation Department.
1924	Son Robert is born.
1928	Fleming becomes Professor of Bacteriology at St Mary's Hospital Medical School; also discovers penicillin.
1929	Fleming presents penicillin studies to Medical Research Council.
1936	Howard Florey and Ernst Boris Chain begin work which will lead them to penicillin.
1939	Outbreak of World War II.
1940	Florey and Chain purify penicillin by vacuum freeze-drying.
1941	Penicillin is first tested on animals and people.
1942	Success of penicillin brings world recognition for Fleming.
1943	Penicillin goes into mass production in the USA.
1944	Fleming is awarded many medals, honours and memberships and is knighted as Sir Alexander Fleming.
1945	World War II ends. Fleming receives many more honours including Nobel Prize jointly with Florey and Chain.

1946	Almroth Wright retires.
	Fleming becomes Principle of the Institute of Bacteriology and begins his trips and tours around the world.
1947	Fleming becomes Director of the Wright-Fleming Institute.
1948	Fleming is appointed Emeritus Professor of Bacteriology at the University of London.
1949	Sarah Fleming dies.
1951	Fleming becomes Lord Rector of the University of Edinburgh. He continues to make trips and tours and receive awards and medals around the world each year.
1953	Fleming marries Amalia Voureka.
1955	Alexander Fleming dies.

Places to visit and further reading

Places to visit

Alexander Fleming Laboratory Museum, St Mary's Hospital, Praed Street, London (The museum is in the very room where Alexander Fleming worked.)

The Wellcome Institute for the History of Medicine, 183 Euston Road, London (One of the world's leading museums on all aspects of medicine.)

Alexander Fleming Memorial Garden, Main Street, Darvel, Ayrshire, Scotland (A garden established in Fleming's memory.)

Websites

The story of Fleming's discovery:
www.pbs.org/wgbh/aso/databank/entries/bmflem.html

Series of features on Fleming, Florey, Chain, the story of penicillin and the development of antibiotics: www.bbc.co.uk/education/medicine

The story of Fleming's life, told from the view of Fleming as a Nobel Prize-winner (Nobel laureate): www.nobel.se/laureates/medicine-1945-1-bio.html

Further reading

Birch, Beverley: *Alexander Fleming* (Exley Publications, 1990)

Gottfried, Ted: *Alexander Fleming: Discoverer of Penicillin* (Franklin Watts, 1997)

Otfinoski, Steven: *Alexander Fleming* (Facts on File Inc., 1993)

Glossary

antibiotic substance that kills or harms other living things

antiseptic substance that is used to clean a wound and make it free from germs

bacteria tiny and simple living things that can be seen through a microscope

bacteriologist expert on bacteria, especially those which cause disease

chemotherapeutic agents chemical substances that treat and cure illness

colonies in bacteria, small patches where millions of them grow and multiply

corn-steep liquor liquid obtained from soaking corn

culture medium substance that provides food and a place to live for small, simple living things

Fellow of the Royal Society important and respected member of a famous British scientific society

gangrene disease in which body flesh goes dark, soft and smelly, and quickly rots away or decays, usually due to bacteria

genetic engineering altering genes by scientific methods in the laboratory

infection when bacteria or other microbes get on to or into the body, multiply and cause disease

inoculation involves giving someone a vaccine, usually by injection. The vaccine contains dead or weakened versions of the bacterial germs, which cause a disease. The body becomes protected or immune to the germs without suffering the disease.

Institute of Bacteriology British scientific organization for the study of bacteria and similar tiny living things, especially those which cause diseases

knighted in Britain, when a person is given the title of 'knight' by the king or queen, and is called Sir rather than Mr. It is a traditional and great honour.

lysozyme natural substance that can break apart or damage certain microbes

Medical Research Council the organization that oversees research into drugs and other medical matters in Britain

microbes microscopic living things

microscopic object that is too small to be seen except under a microscope

mucus slimy substance that protects body surfaces such as the insides of the nose and throat

Nobel prize one of six awards offered each year for great achievement, the six topics being physics, chemistry, physiology or medicine, literature, economics and promotion of peace

oculist doctor who specializes in eye problems

Pasteur Institute scientific organization based in Paris, which looks into the causes and effects of disease and the general study of microbes

pathology study of the effects of illness and disease on the body

penicillin natural substance made by *Penicillium*, that works as an antibiotic

Penicillium type of fungus or mould that produces the antibiotic penicillin

phagocytosis (you say 'fag-owe-sigh-toe-sis') when a microscopic living thing, such as a white cell in the blood, 'eats' an item such as an invading bacterium

pneumonia severe chest illness which affects the lungs

preceptors people who teach, instruct or educate

Rocky Mountain spotted fever infection where the body becomes hot and sweaty and the skin develops a rash

Royal College of Surgeons organization in London, working for progress in the detection and treatment of illness and disease, by surgery

Royal Institute of Medicine organization working for progress in the detection and treatment of illness and disease by various medical methods

septicaemia 'blood poisoning', when microbes get into the blood and spread around the body and multiply to cause serious illness

sexually transmitted diseases illnesses or diseases spread by various forms of sexual contact

smallpox severe illness causing fever, sores, scars and sometimes death

spores tiny seed-like parts produced by moulds and similar living things, found in air, soil and water

Staphylococcus types of bacteria which are rounded or ball-shaped and which cause skin boils, sore throats and similar problems

Streptomyces common type of mould or fungus that lives in the soil

streptomycin antibiotic substance produced by the mould *Streptomyces*

suspension tiny particles floating in a liquid

syphilis serious sexually transmitted disease caused by bacterial microbes

tetanus serious disease caused by infection with bacterial microbes that live in places associated with 'dirt', such as the soil

transfusion medical treatment when blood or fluid is put into the body

vaccines substances containing disease-causing microbes (or their products) in dead or weakened form. They are put into the body by inoculation, during the process of vaccination, and prepare the body to protect itself against those microbes in the future

vacuum freeze-drying when a mixture of substances is frozen solid, then gently warmed while in a vacuum (airless place) to obtain one of the substances in pure form

virus microscopic agent that invades cells of an animal and causes infection

X-ray invisible rays used in medicine used to detect diseases inside the body

Index